# HEALTHY BODY

# Harmful Substances

Text by Carol Ballard • Photography by Robert Pickett

BLACKBIRCH®
PRESS

THOMSON

GALE

San Diego • Detroit • New York • San Francisco • Cleveland • New Haven, Conn. • Waterville, Maine • London • Munich

TITLES IN THE HEALTHY BODY SERIES:

# • Personal Hygiene • Eating Right • Safety • Exercise • Relationships • Harmful Substances

## THOMSON
## GALE

© 2004 by White-Thompson Publishing Ltd.

Produced by White-Thompson Publishing Ltd.
2/3 St. Andrew's Place
Lewes BN7 1UP, U.K.

*For more information, contact*
The Gale Group, Inc.
27500 Drake Rd.
Farmington Hills, MI 48331-3535
Or you can visit our Internet site at http://www.gale.com

Editor:              Elaine Fuoco-Lang

Consultant:          Chris Sculthorpe, East Sussex,
                     Brighton & Hove Healthy School
                     Scheme Co-ordinator

Inside design:       Joelle Wheelwright

Cover design:        Hodder Wayland

Photographs:         Robert Pickett

Proofreader:         Jane Colgan

Artwork:             Peter Bull

Acknowledgements:
The publishers would like to thank the following
for their assistance with this book: the staff
and children of Salmestone Primary School, Margate,
Kent, UK.

Originally published by Hodder Wayland,
an imprint of Hodder Children's Books,
a division of Hodder Headline Limited
338 Euston Road, London NW1 3BH

Picture acknowledgements:
Angela Hampton Family Picture Library 4, 5 top, 9 top, 13 top, 15 top, 18 bottom, 20 bottom, 21 bottom, 22 top, 28; CORBIS 10 bottom, 13 bottom, 14 top, Jeff Albertson 23 bottom, Andrew Brookes 22 bottom, Jim Cummins 29 top; Robert Essel NYC 18 top, Paul Hardy 19 top, Richard Hutchings 17 top, Julius 16, Ronnie Kaufman 20 top and 29 bottom, Lester Lefkowiz 25 top, Roy Morsch 23 top, Mug Shots 26 top, Anna Palma 19 bottom, Steve Starr 25 bottom, Eye Ubiquitous 24 top; Hodder Wayland Picture Library 8 top, 11 top, 12 bottom, 27; Hodder Wayland Picture Library/Chris Fairclough 7; Robert Pickett 6 top, 8 bottom, 9 bottom, 10 top, 11 bottom, 14 bottom, 17 bottom, 21 top, 24 bottom; Simon Fraser/ Science Photo Library 12 top; WTPix 5 bottom, 6 bottom, 15 bottom.

The photographs in this book are of models who have granted their permission for their use in this title.

**LIBRARY OF CONGRESS CATALOGING-IN-PUBLICATION DATA**

Ballard, Carol.
    Harmful substances / by Carol Ballard.
       p. cm. — (Healthy body)
    Includes bibliographical references and index.
    Contents: What are harmful substances?—Everyday substances—Medicines—Smoking—How does smoking harm your body?—Alcohol—Alcohol and behavior—How does alcohol harm your body?—Solvents—Ecstasy and marijuana—Heroin and cocaine—What is addiction?—How to keep safe.
    ISBN 1-4103-0163-X (hardback : alk. paper)
    1. Toxicology—Juvenile literature. [1. Toxicology. 2. Toxins.] I. Title. II. Series.
    RA1214.B35 2004
    615.9—dc22
                                                    2003013331

Printed in China
10 9 8 7 6 5 4 3 2 1

# Contents

# What are harmful substances?

It is good to know that our homes, schools, and other places we go are safe and that we are unlikely to come to any harm. All around us, though, are things that could hurt us. Most of the time we are protected from them. There are times, though, when you need to be responsible for your own safety and know what to do to look after yourself.

▲ *We usually feel safe at home with our families.*

There are many different types of harmful substances. Some, like cleaning materials, are everyday things that many people have in their homes. You may see adults using others, such as alcohol and cigarettes. These substances may seem safe, but they can have hidden dangers. Medicines may be harmful if taken in the wrong amounts and by the wrong people. Other harmful substances include drugs that you may have heard about, such as marijuana, ecstasy, heroin, and cocaine.

▲ *Alcohol may seem safe, but it does have risks.*

▼ *Being aware of possible dangers can help you make sensible decisions that will keep you healthy and safe.*

# Everyday substances

Most people keep a range of different cleaning materials, such as bleach and disinfectant, in their homes. These are very useful, but they can make you very ill if you swallow them. Some can also cause burns if they touch your skin. Some give off fumes that can hurt your lungs and make it difficult to breathe. Do not use substances like these unless an adult has told you to, and always read the safety warnings on the label.

▲ **Oven cleaner contains chemicals that can cause harm if the product is used incorrectly.**

Many people use chemicals in their yards. Weed killers do not only kill weeds. They also give you a very bad stomachache if you swallow them, and you may need a trip to the hospital. Other substances, such as insect sprays and fertilizers, are bad for you too, so stay well away from them.

▲ **Some gardening products contain harmful chemicals.**

If you do accidentally swallow something you should not or spill something on your skin, tell an adult right away. He or she can make sure you get the help and first aid that you need.

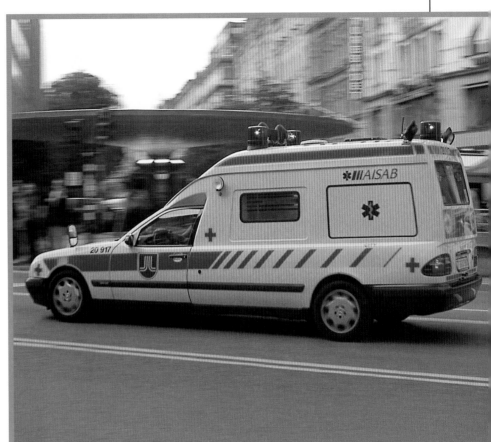

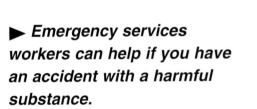

▶ *Emergency services workers can help if you have an accident with a harmful substance.*

## Fantastic Facts

It makes sense to keep substances that could harm people in their original containers. Special signs on bottles and other containers act as a code to tell people whether the contents are dangerous or not. Some of the signs are:

● a skull and crossbones, which means "POISON"

● a flame, which means "will easily catch fire"

● an X, which means "will irritate skin"

Tankers carrying chemicals have these signs on them. If there is an accident and the contents are spilled, emergency services will know what to do.

# Medicines

Medicines are substances that are taken to help your body recover from illness. All medicines are drugs—substances that, when they enter your body, have an effect on you or on the way you feel. Medicines can be very powerful and, if not taken properly, can be dangerous. Whenever a doctor writes a prescription, he or she makes sure that the medicine is correct for the patient. The medicine itself, or the amount of it, may be totally wrong and possibly harmful for someone else. Never be tempted to take somebody else's medicine, even if it looks exactly the same as your own. Medicines always have information about how much should be taken, and how often.

▲ *If you are unsure about how to take your medicine, ask an adult for help.*

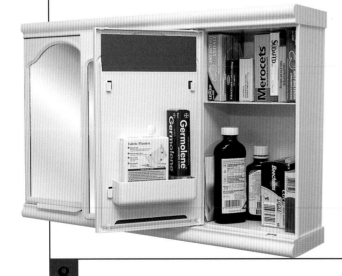

There may be instructions about when to take medicine, such as before or after a meal, just before you go to bed, or when you first wake up. It is important to follow all these instructions carefully so that the medicine can work properly.

◄ *Medicine labels tell you how to use the medicine. Always follow these instructions exactly.*

Not all drugs are medicines, though. Some drugs affect your body and the way you feel, but they harm your body rather than helping it. This includes some common substances such as nicotine and alcohol, as well as other more dangerous substances.

Some everyday things like coffee and chocolate can also affect your body and how you feel. Unless you consume huge amounts, though, they are unlikely to do you any harm.

◄ *Even chocolate can affect how you feel.*

 ## Healthy Hints

Sometimes, we may take medicines when we do not actually need them. This is not a good idea. Our bodies may get used to them so that when we are really ill, they do not work as well. Often, if you feel unwell, perhaps with a stomachache or headache, a quiet rest will do as much good as medicine.

▲ *If you feel unwell, resting is often a good idea.*

# Smoking

People smoke for many different reasons. For some, smoking is a habit that they have had for many years and cannot break. Some young people start to smoke to copy other people. Others are persuaded to start by friends who are smokers. Some young people think that smoking makes them look grown up, or helps them become part of a group.

▲ **Smoking is harmful to your body no matter what your age.**

Cigarettes are made from the crushed, dried leaves of tobacco plants, held together by a strip of paper. Some have a plug of material, called a filter, at one end. As the cigarette burns, the leaves produce chemicals and gases.

◄ **The leaves from tobacco plants are used to make cigarettes.**

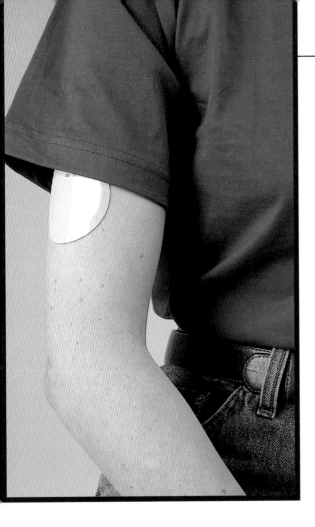

Smokers become addicted to nicotine, one of the chemicals produced when tobacco is burned. This means that they need to keep smoking to keep getting more nicotine.

Scientists have tried to find ways to make it easier to give up smoking. Nicotine patches stick on the skin and release tiny amounts of nicotine into the body. This is just enough to keep the person from wanting another cigarette. Chewing gum that contains nicotine can also help.

**◄ A nicotine patch can help a person quit smoking.**

## 🍎 Healthy Hints

Many smokers find that they become very irritable when they try to give up their cigarettes. They often feel nervous and anxious. Some eat a lot of sweets instead, and some find that they start to put on weight. It makes good sense never to start smoking because then you will never have to battle to give it up!

**► Nicotine in cigarettes makes smoking difficult to give up.**

# How does smoking harm your body?

Nicotine is a chemical produced when tobacco is burned. It is addictive. That means that it acts as a drug, and smokers find it hard to live without it. They say that it helps them to relax and stay calm. It may do these things—but it has other effects, too. Nicotine makes the heart beat more quickly. It makes the blood vessels narrower, so the heart has to work harder to pump blood around the body. Nicotine also makes the stomach produce more acid, which can lead to stomach ulcers.

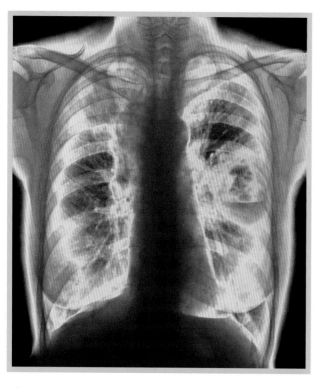

▲ **This X-ray shows that smoking has caused this person to develop lung cancer.**

Burning tobacco also produces a sticky brown liquid called tar. This gets into the lungs when you breathe in cigarette smoke. It can clog up the narrow passages in the lungs, making breathing difficult. It can also damage the lungs themselves, causing diseases such as lung cancer.

▶ **Tar collects in your lungs if you smoke.**

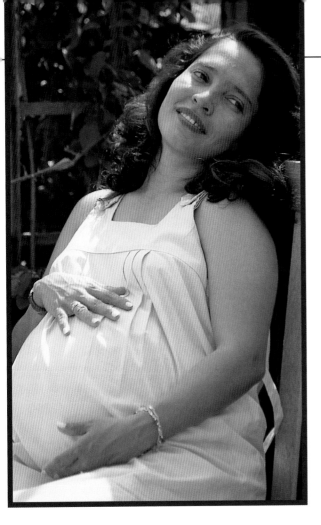

Cigarette smoke can make you look and smell unpleasant. Yellow-stained fingers, yellow-tinged hair, wrinkly skin, brown teeth, and bad breath can all result from smoking cigarettes.

If a woman smokes while she is pregnant, it can harm her unborn baby. Babies born to mothers who smoke are more likely to be underweight and suffer from infections than babies born to mothers who do not smoke.

◀ *Smoking can harm everyone, including unborn children.*

## \!?/ Fantastic Facts

Have you ever looked across a room filled with the smoky haze of cigarette smoke? Even if you do not smoke, sitting in a smoky room means that the air you breathe contains some of the chemicals and gases produced from burning cigarettes. This is called passive smoking. Scientists and doctors have learned that passive smoking causes illness in nonsmokers just as cigarettes cause illness in smokers.

▶ *No-smoking areas are becoming increasingly common.*

# Alcohol

Alcohol is a drug that many people say makes them feel relaxed, happy, and confident. Many adults enjoy drinking alcohol. In small quantities, it will not harm them. Some, though, drink too much alcohol too often, and this can cause a lot of damage to their bodies.

▶ *Many adults enjoy drinking alcohol.*

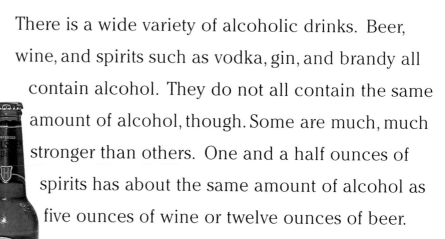

There is a wide variety of alcoholic drinks. Beer, wine, and spirits such as vodka, gin, and brandy all contain alcohol. They do not all contain the same amount of alcohol, though. Some are much, much stronger than others. One and a half ounces of spirits has about the same amount of alcohol as five ounces of wine or twelve ounces of beer.

◀ *Spirits such as whiskey and vodka contain much more alcohol than beer.*

Some drinks can be misleading. They may look like ordinary juices and sodas, but they can contain a lot of alcohol. You might be tempted to try them, but it is better to avoid them.

► *It is better for you to have a soft drink than one containing alcohol.*

 **Fantastic Facts**

Strict laws control who can sell alcohol, buy it and drink it, and when and where it can be sold, bought, and drunk. In the United States, the minimum drinking age in every state is twenty-one.

◄ *You do not need to drink alcohol to have a great time.*

# Alcohol and behavior

Alcohol is often thought to cheer you up, but the drug really slows the body down so that you begin to lose control. There is a delay of just a few minutes between drinking alcohol and the alcohol reaching the brain. At first, it may produce a feeling of happiness and relaxation. As more is consumed, the heart beats faster. Vision, speech, and balance are all affected and the person seems "drunk." The person slowly loses control and may do things that he or she would never dream of doing normally. He or she may be very ashamed and embarrassed about the behavior later.

▲ *It can be tempting to drink with your friends. Drinking, though, can make you act differently and feel unwell.*

Lots of trouble can be caused by groups of young adults who have drunk too much alcohol. They may be noisy, behave badly, and may get in trouble with the police for upsetting other people or for damaging cars, buildings, and other things. The results of what may have begun as an evening's fun can be serious and long-term.

◄ *A police officer in Florida checks that a driver has not been drinking by watching him walk along a straight line. If you have been drinking, your balance becomes affected.*

## ⎰⎱— Action Zone

Alcohol slows your reaction to things that happen around you. Since reaction time is important when driving, it is illegal in many places to drive after drinking. Test your reaction time:

1. Ask a friend to hold a ruler in the air, with "12 in" at the top.

2. Without actually touching the ruler, hold your thumb and first finger at the "0". Watch carefully. When the friend lets go, try to catch the ruler as quickly as you can. Read the number to see how many inches the ruler fell before you caught it. The smaller the number, the faster your reaction time.

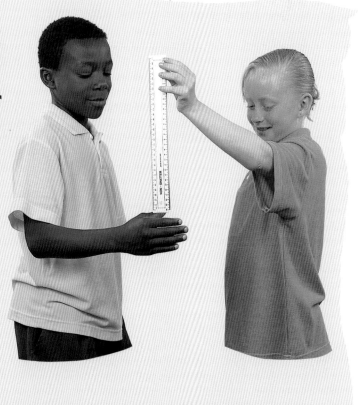

▲ *How quick are your reactions?*

# How does alcohol harm your body?

Alcohol affects your body in several ways. Some effects are swift, while others take longer to develop. Alcohol slows down the messages passing between the brain and the rest of the body. This makes it harder to control speech, vision, and balance. Alcohol irritates the lining of the stomach, causing nausea and vomiting. Excess alcohol may cause a person to lose consciousness and, in extreme cases, alcohol poisoning may lead to death.

▲ **Drinking too much alcohol can make you feel unwell.**

◀ **Drinking can make some people depressed.**

After drinking a lot of alcohol, a person may suffer from a hangover the next day. This usually means having a bad headache and feeling tired and sick.

Drinking too much over a long period can have a bad effect on a person's health. Alcohol is high in calories, so many heavy drinkers are overweight. The blood pressure may be raised, and heart muscle damaged. The brain may also deteriorate. The liver removes alcohol from the blood, so too much alcohol can cause damage to the liver. Continued heavy drinking can lead to liver failure and death.

▲ *Heavy drinking, as well as overeating, can cause obesity.*

## \!?/ Fantastic Facts

If a woman drinks alcohol while she is pregnant, it may harm her unborn baby. The alcohol in the mother's blood can pass to the baby, slowing down the rate at which it grows. Alcohol may also damage the baby's brain, and may prevent other organs, such as the eyes, from developing properly.

▶ *Pregnant women should avoid alcohol.*

# Solvents

Have you ever noticed the distinctive smell as you pass a dry cleaner? That is an example of a solvent smell. Solvents are chemicals that give off strong gases.

▶ **Solvents are used when clothes are dry-cleaned.**

Many solvents are used in substances such as glues, lighter fuel, cleaning fluids, and some aerosols.

They can be used safely for their intended purpose, as long as the safety precautions are followed carefully. Used wrongly though, solvents can kill.

◀ **Solvents are used in correction fluid. Always use correction fluid in a well-ventilated area.**

# \?/ Fantastic Facts

Stores that sell glue and similar products may have signs saying that it is illegal to sell solvents to children and teenagers. The age limits may vary from one country to another, but the penalties for stores that break the law are usually severe. This is because governments all recognize how dangerous solvents can be.

► *Products that contain solvents can be dangerous if they are not used correctly.*

Some people sniff, or inhale, solvents. This is extremely dangerous. A single cigarette or alcoholic drink is unlikely to kill you, but just one whiff of a solvent might. People inhale the gas from solvents because they like the feeling of lightheadedness and dizziness that it gives them. Some say it makes them feel happy and excited. Some even squirt the solvent into their mouths. Never be tempted to misuse solvents. You can die almost immediately from heart failure or suffocation.

◄ *Some people get others to buy solvents for them. Inhaling solvents is very dangerous.*

# Ecstasy and marijuana

Ecstasy is a drug that is becoming increasingly used by young people, especially at places like nightclubs. It is also known as "E" or "XTC."

Ecstasy is usually taken as a tablet. People say it makes them feel very happy and more aware of what is happening around them than usual. They may also feel warm and friendly toward other people.

▲ *Even if people you know take drugs, you should never feel you have to do the same.*

Ecstasy can have severe side effects, though. People who take it may feel like dancing for hours at a time without rest or water. This makes their bodies overheat. They may collapse, or have a heat stroke. Some scientists believe that using Ecstasy over time can cause brain damage.

◀ *Ecstasy is a dangerous drug.*

Marijuana has a lot of other names, including pot, grass, and dope. It is made from the dried leaves of the cannabis plant and looks like dried grass. Most people who use it roll it up and smoke it like a cigarette. The leaves of the cannabis plant can also be used and baked with food. People who use marijuana say it helps them relax and calm down. Using it, however, can make it harder to do well at school. It

▲ *Marijuana is made from the leaves of the cannabis plant.*

may affect your concentration, your memory, and your ability to get yourself to the right place at the right time. Although using marijuana is unlikely to kill you, it can cause problems in your everyday life. Some scientists think that using it may lead to mental health problems.

 **Fantastic Facts**

Some people think that doctors should be allowed to prescribe marijuana as a medicine for particular patients. People suffering from diseases such as multiple sclerosis often find that marijuana can help control the symptoms of their illness and make them feel much better. In most states, though, using marijuana is still illegal.

► *A woman holds a pipe for smoking prescribed medical marijuana.*

# Heroin and cocaine

Heroin is made from opium poppy plants. It can be smoked, but is more usually injected. People say it makes them feel warm and comfortable, but there can be unpleasant side effects such as nausea and headaches.

Heroin is known by many different names, including smack, skag, and junk. It is usually found as a white or brown powder. It is illegal to use heroin in many countries, including the United States.

► *Poppies can be used to make opium.*

▼ *Heroin is usually injected with needles.*

One of the main problems with heroin is that it is extremely addictive. This means that once a person has used it, he or she will probably want to use it again. They become used to it, and then find it difficult to live without. Heroin is very expensive, so many people end up stealing and getting involved with other crimes in order to pay for it.

Users often share needles when injecting heroin. They may also use needles that have been used before and may not be sterile. This means that diseases can easily be passed from one person to another.

▲ **Cocaine is a very addictive drug**

Cocaine is a white, powdery substance. It has several other names, including coke, snow, and stardust. People who use cocaine say it makes them feel alert and very happy. Afterwards, though, they often feel sad and nervous.

Cocaine is usually taken by sniffing it into the nostrils. It is very addictive, so once a person takes cocaine, he or she is likely to want more and more. Sniffing cocaine slowly destroys the inside of the nose, leaving the face disfigured and ugly.

Crack cocaine is a very strong, very pure form of cocaine. It is even more dangerous than ordinary cocaine. It is usually taken by smoking.

# Fantastic Facts

Opium poppies are grown abroad, and the heroin they produce is smuggled into other countries. Cocaine is often smuggled from one country to another as well. Police and other officials from different countries work together to try to stop the trade. The laws in most countries mean there are long prison sentences and, in some places, even execution for people involved in smuggling heroin and cocaine.

▲ **Officials use drug-sniffing dogs to search for illegal drugs.**

# What is addiction?

Addiction means needing something and not being able to give it up. Drug addicts are unable to manage without regular doses of a drug, even though they may know they are harming themselves by taking it.

▲ *Drug addiction can result in a lot of trouble.*

## Healthy Hints

It can be difficult to know what to do if you are offered something you do not want to take. Here are some suggestions:

● Stay cool, calm, and confident. Say no, and stick to it.

● Keep repeating the same answer, such as, "I don't take drugs."

● Ignore the offer—talk about something else.

● If people start to taunt you, avoid arguing. Say something like "O.K." or "Whatever."

● Tell an adult you trust as soon as you can.

Addiction can really mess up a person's life. Most drugs damage the body in some way. Many affect the mind as well. Addicts often skip school, college, and other important things so they end up doing less well than other people. Many addicts cannot afford the drugs they need, so they steal to pay for them. They often find themselves in trouble with the police.

Having an addict in the family is very difficult for everybody. The addict's behavior may make the rest of the family feel awkward, embarrassed, or ashamed. Parents may want to help, but may not know what to do. Younger brothers and sisters can be upset and influenced by the addict's behavior and attitudes.

► *Taking drugs may make you feel happy at the time. Afterward, though, it can make you feel extremely low.*

Many organizations try to help addicts recover from their addictions. It is often very difficult, though, for an addict to accept that he or she needs help. Talking over the situation, discussing what went wrong and why, and making changes one small step at a time can all help an addict overcome his or her addiction.

◄ *If you are worried about a friend, remember to talk to an adult.*

# How to keep safe

The most important thing you need to do as you grow up is keep yourself safe. One of the ways to do this is to avoid harmful substances. The hints on page 26 suggest ways in which you can avoid substances you do not want to take. You can also keep yourself safe by avoiding places where you might be offered things. For example, if you know that a group of teenagers often hangs around a particular street corner and smokes, then plan your route so that you do not have to go past them.

▲ *Stay away from people who use peer pressure to cause trouble.*

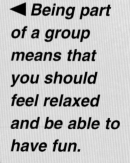

◄ *Being part of a group means that you should feel relaxed and be able to have fun.*

You can help keep your brothers, sisters, friends, and classmates safe, too, by being alert. Some of the signs that a person might be using a harmful substance include:

● sudden mood changes

● being sleepy and unable to concentrate

● being secretive and lying

● not being interested in things he or she used to like, such as sports and other hobbies

● not taking as much care of himself or herself as he or she used to.

You should always tell an adult you trust if you think someone may have a substance problem. Remember, though, that all of these signs can also be just a normal part of growing up. They do not necessarily mean that there is a problem.

▲ **Have fun without drugs.**

## ∿ **Action Zone**

If you suspect or know that someone close to you—a brother or sister, friend, or classmate—has a substance problem, tell an adult you trust as soon as you can. You may think that this is tattling, but it is not. Anybody who has a substance problem needs help. The sooner they get it, the sooner they can start to recover. By telling an adult about it, you are helping to begin that recovery process for them.

▶ *Telling an adult can help sort out a friend's problems.*

# Glossary

**addict** a person who needs regular doses of a substance.

**alcohol** a drug that many people enjoy as a drink.

**alcohol poisoning** the result of too much alcohol in the blood for the body to cope.

**anxious** worrying about something.

**blood vessels** the tubes through which blood flows around the body.

**drug** a substance that affects the body and how we feel.

**hangover** the after-effects of drinking too much alcohol.

**irritate** to cause discomfort.

**lungs** the organs used for breathing.

**medical marijuana** marijuana prescribed by a doctor to treat illness.

**medicine** a drug that helps cure an illness.

**nausea** a feeling of sickness.

**nervous** frightened or worried.

**nicotine** a chemical in tobacco that is very addictive.

**passive smoking** breathing in smoke from another person's cigarette.

**responsible** to be in control of.

**solvent** a chemical that gives off strong-smelling gases.

# For more information

Chier, Ruth, *Inhalants.* New York: Rosen, 2003.

Graves, Bonnie, *Alcohol Use and Abuse.* Mankato, MN: Capstone, 2000.

Kreiner, Anna, *Let's Talk About Drug Abuse.* New York: Rosen, 2003.

Picard, E. Rafaela, *Drugs in Your Neighborhood.* New York: Rosen, 2003.

Robbins, Paul, *Crack and Cocaine Drug Dangers.* Berkeley Heights, NJ: Enslow, 2001.

Sevastiades, Patra McSharry, *Heroin.* New York: Rosen, 2003.

Silverstein, Alvin, *Poison.* New York: Scholastic, 2003.

————, *Smoking.* New York: Scholastic, 2003.

Sloan, Julie, *Why Do People Drink Alcohol?* Austin, TX: Raintree, 2001.

Stewart, Gail B., *Drugs.* San Diego: KidHaven, 2002.

————, *Smoking.* San Diego: KidHaven, 2003.

# Index

All page numbers in **bold** refer to pictures as well as text